(Hesperis matronalis, L.)

Fig 58

For Frances, who believed in this story
and stayed with me to the end
—C.R.

For my mom, who taught me to draw
and nurtured a love for early American history
—J.C.

ACKNOWLEDGMENTS

Heartfelt thanks go to the following people for their assistance in the research and fact-checking for this book:
Anna Berkes, Research Librarian, Jefferson Library, Charlottesville, Virginia; Emilie Johnson, Assistant Curator,
Thomas Jefferson Foundation, Charlottesville, Virginia; Keith Thomson, former Executive Officer, American
Philosophical Society, Philadelphia, and author of many books on paleontology and Thomas Jefferson; Ross MacPhee,
Curator, Department of Mammalogy, Division of Vertebrate Zoology, American Museum of Natural History, New
York; and Harry R. Haynes, former Manager, Museum of the Middle Appalachians, Saltville, Virginia.

Library of Congress Cataloging-in-Publication Data is available upon request.
ISBN 978-0-525-64607-5 (trade) — ISBN 978-0-525-64608-2 (lib. bdg.) — ISBN 978-0-525-64609-9 (ebook)

The artist used ink drawings, colored digitally, to create the illustrations for this book.
The text is set in P22 Franklin Caslon, based on letters made by Benjamin Franklin's printing office around 1750
and reflecting eighteenth-century textured paper and handmade ink.
Interior design by Elizabeth Tardiff

MANUFACTURED IN CHINA
10 9 8 7 6 5 4 3 2 1
First Edition

Bones
in the
White House

THOMAS JEFFERSON'S MAMMOTH

by Candice Ransom

illustrated by Jamey Christoph

Doubleday Books for Young Readers

Long ago, tales like campfire smoke drifted across America. They hinted of a monster roaming territories west of the Mississippi River.

Thomas Jefferson heard those stories. Surveyors, traders, and trappers staggered back from the wilds of Kentucky with enormous tusks and thrilling accounts of massive bones scattered on the ground.

Huge ribs and shoulder blades stuck up from the blue-gray muck, they said. One man reported using gigantic bones as tent poles and stools.

In 1781, America was still mostly vast wilderness. No one in the East knew what mysterious animals might wander in the far West.

Jefferson was enthralled. What brute could have left behind such mighty skeletons? He itched to see those bones.

He had always been curious. As a boy, he picked up shells as old as the rocks in the Blue Ridge Mountains. He wondered how relics of sea life came to rest on a mountaintop in Virginia.

That curious country boy grew up to write the Declaration of Independence and was governor of Virginia while America fought Britain to gain its freedom.

But after
America won the
war, some across the
Atlantic felt the former
colony had little to offer.
Jefferson knew the truth—
and these giant bones would
help him prove it. He decided
to write a book that would tell the
world America was a great country, full
of great creatures. But describing an animal
no living person had seen would not be easy.

At the American Philosophical Society, where Jefferson and other men interested in science would meet, some believed the colossal tusks and leg bones being dug up out West belonged to an elephant. Some thought the whopping teeth belonged to a hippopotamus. Others argued the animal was both elephant *and* hippopotamus.

In fact, it was a *mastodon*, but in Jefferson's time it became known as a *mammoth*, after a similar creature that had been dug up in Siberia. In his book, Jefferson listed the mammoth along with moose, mountain lions, buffalo, and bears. He wrote that the newly discovered, mysterious "large-big" creature "still exists in the northern parts of America."

NOTES

ON THE

STATE OF VIRGINIA

WITH AN

APPENDIX.

BY THOMAS JEFFERSON.

NOTES ON VIRGINIA
II. *Aboriginals of one only.*

EUROPE.			AMERICA.	
Sanglier.	Wild boar	lb.		lb.
Mouflon.	Wild sheep	280.		
Bouquentin.	Wildgoat	56.	Tapir	
Lievre.	Hare		Elk. round horned	534.
Lapin.	Rabbit	7.6	Puma	+450.
Putois.	Polecat	3.4	Jugar	
Genette		3.3	Cabiai	218.
Defman.		3.1	Tamanoire	109.
Equreuil.	Muscrat	oz.	Tammandua	109.
Hermine.	Squirrel.	12.	Cougar of N.America	65.
Rat.	Ermin	8.2	Cougar of S.America	75.4
Loirs.	Rat.	7.5	Ocelot	59.
Lerot.		3.1	Pecari	
Taupe.	Dormouse	1.8	Jaguaret	46.3
Hamster.	Mole	1.2	Alco	43.6
Zifel.		.9	Lama	
Leming.		.9	Paco	
Souris.	Mouse		Paca	
		.6	Serval	
			Sloth. Unau	32.7
			Saricovienne	27.25
			Kinkajou	
			Tatou Kabassou	
			Urso. Urchin	21.8
			Racoon. Raton	
			Coati	16.5
			Coendou	
			Sloth.	
			Sapajou Ai	16.3
			Tatou Ourini	13.
			Tateu Encubert	9.8
			Tatou Apar	
			Little Cachica	
			Opossum. Coendou	7.
			Sarigue	6.5

He added a chart listing the weights of American mammals. The space for the mammoth's weight was blank. How much did an unknown animal weigh?
If only he could get his hands on a mammoth bone, he could figure it out.

Many of his friends owned bones from Big Bone Lick, a salty bog near the Ohio River in Kentucky. Prehistoric animals had come to lick the salt from the mud, gotten stuck, and died. George Washington had a leg bone and a molar. Benjamin Franklin possessed several specimens. Even the king of France displayed a femur, teeth, and a tusk in his private museum.

Jefferson had no bones. Only a bad case of "mammoth fever."

Jefferson's friend George Rogers Clark lived near Big Bone Lick. "Were it possible to get a tooth," he told Clark, "it would particularly oblige me." General Clark tried to collect a thigh bone, but it broke as he dug it up. Offering to pay, Jefferson asked for *any* bones Clark could find. When the general hiked to the Lick again, the ground was frozen solid. Nothing would budge.

Word spread about Jefferson's keen interest in the mystery animal. He was given a jumbo tooth that came from a salt marsh in southwestern Virginia. It was studded with cone-shaped points.

Jefferson marveled at its heaviness and shape. Elephant molars, he knew, were flat-topped for grinding plants. Was the mammoth a carnivore? He pictured great meat-eating beasts stampeding through his native state.

He must have more bones!

General Clark sent Jefferson a thigh bone.
It was as tall as a three-year-old child! Yet this
first bone only fanned his mammoth fever.
If he had a *whole* skeleton, he would know
what the creature looked like.

In the spring of 1796, Jefferson received a package of fossils from a friend. It held strange leg and foot bones and—oddest of all—toe bones with giant claws.

The fossils did not belong to Jefferson's hoped-for mammoth, but a new beast he named "Great-claw" in a scientific essay. Jefferson thought the animal must be a wild cat, three times bigger than a lion. He felt certain this giant cat prowled uncharted forests, along with the mammoth.

In 1797, Jefferson was elected vice president of the United States and president of the American Philosophical Society. He traveled to Philadelphia to accept both offices, carrying with him the Great-claw bones and his essay. It was an honor to be vice president, yet he was more excited to reveal his scientific discovery.

Society members blasted his ideas. Without a thigh bone, how could he know the size of the Great-claw? Why hadn't anyone ever *seen* one?

MEGALONYX JEFFERSONII

Jefferson didn't back down. Even when he learned he had been wrong, and that the Great-claw bones actually belonged to an ancient sloth, he believed in the *possibility* of more discoveries. If the mammoth wandered somewhere in the West, what *else* might be out there?

As Society president, Jefferson pushed the "Bone Committee" to step up its research.

They needed bones. Lots of them.

Then, in 1799, a worker on John Masten's farm in Newburgh, New York, stabbed his shovel into the ground. It struck something hard. The bones of a monster. *Lots* of them.

Jefferson tried to buy the Masten bones. The farmer refused to sell.

The following year, Jefferson became the third president of the United States. He moved into the President's House, a grand new home on Pennsylvania Avenue in Washington, DC, which later became known as the White House.

But he didn't forget about his mammoth. A complete skeleton would draw worldwide attention to America's natural wonders.

At Jefferson's urging, a fellow Society member, Charles Willson Peale, went to the Masten farm, where he was successful in buying the bones.

Peale returned to Philadelphia to assemble the skeleton, adding wooden parts in place of the missing skull top and lower jaw. It measured seventeen feet long and eleven feet high at the shoulder, weighing over a thousand pounds!

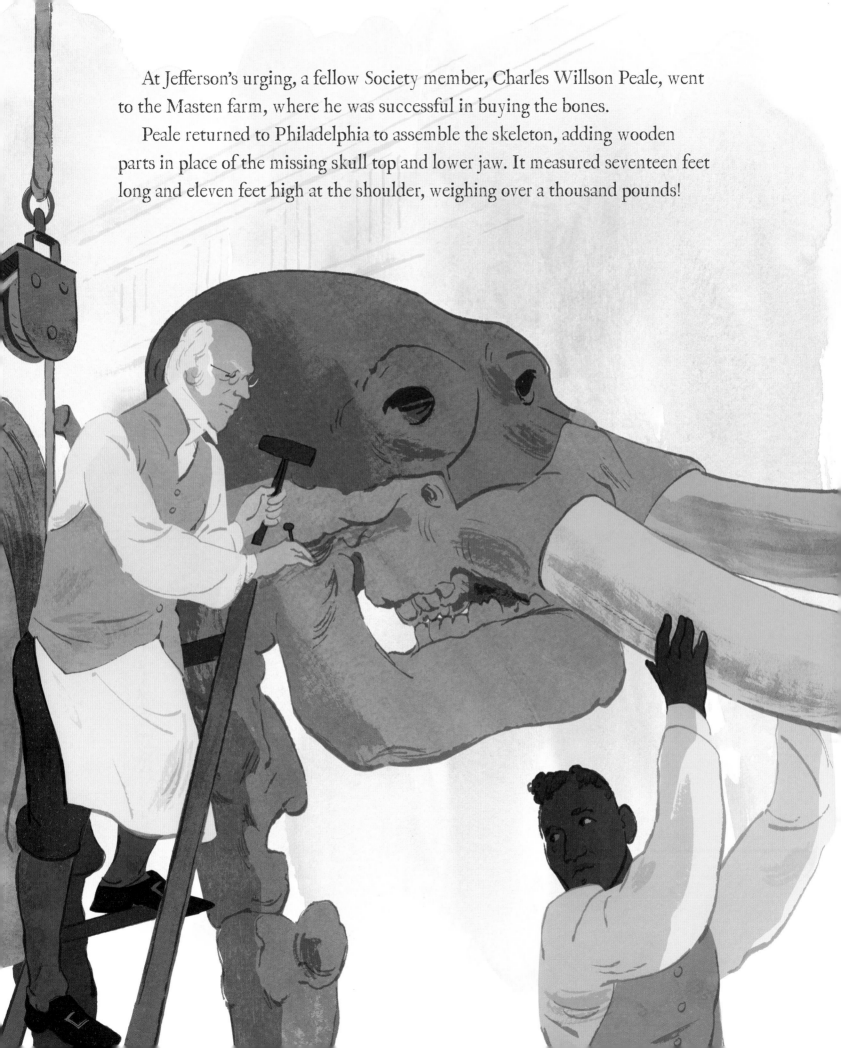

On Christmas Day 1801, the mammoth stood in a special room of the American Philosophical Society building. Lit by oil lamps after dark, the hulking creature dwarfed a tiny mouse skeleton posed by its foot to highlight the monster's bulk.

LARGEST
— of —
TERRESTRIAL
BEINGS

People flocked to see the astounding attraction. For seventy-five cents, they could gawk at—as Peale's poster trumpeted—the bones of the "LARGEST of TERRESTRIAL BEINGS."

Suddenly the whole country caught "mammoth fever"! Anything oversized was branded "mammoth."

Newspapers sprouted accounts of a twenty-pound "mammoth radish," "mammoth bread" for sale, and a "mammoth eater," a man who devoured forty-two eggs in ten minutes.

Townspeople in Cheshire, Massachusetts, sent
Jefferson a "mammoth cheese," weighing 1,235 pounds.
On New Year's Day 1802, Jefferson opened his house
to the public. He greeted the cheese-nibbling visitors,
but his thoughts turned west. The United States
needed room to grow, he believed.

And it soon would. With the 1803 Louisiana Purchase—
828,000 square miles sold by France to America—the country
doubled in size, becoming a mammoth nation.

In 1804, Jefferson
sent Meriwether Lewis
and William Clark to
explore the West. *Bring
back bones*, he instructed
them. *And keep an eye
out for a living mammoth.*

Jefferson asked Lewis to stop at Big Bone Lick
on the way, and send back bones that had recently
been dug up. But the boat carrying the fossils to
Washington wrecked, and Jefferson's bones sank to
the bottom of the Mississippi River.

By now, his political enemies jeeringly called him Mr. Mammoth. Jefferson didn't care. When Lewis and Clark returned, he sent Clark to Big Bone Lick to look one more time.

Clark's first report was disappointing. The salt marsh had been picked over by fossil hunters. But his next report glowed with good news. He had collected three hundred bones and teeth! What's more, they were on their way to Washington!

On March 7, 1808, three crates arrived at the President's House. Jefferson had them opened in the East Room, where former First Lady Abigail Adams had once hung laundry. This was now the Bone Room!

Jefferson spread out more than three hundred fossils on the floor. Some belonged to other animal species, but most were from mammoths. Teeth, tusks—one ten feet long!—ribs, leg and foot bones, *and* four jaw bones and four pieces of skulls. All the bones of the American mammoth had now been found.

At the end of his second presidential term, Jefferson retired and went home to Virginia. For years, he'd dreamed of building a university with the study of science at its heart. The foothills of the Blue Ridge Mountains, where mammoths once lumbered, would be a good place.

Thomas Jefferson died in 1826, a year after making his dream come true. His grandson donated most of Jefferson's fossils to the new University of Virginia. Sometime in the middle of the century, however, the bones were lost. There is no record of them after 1848, and to this day, no one knows the location of his collection.

Maybe someday a student will stumble on a dusty box labeled *Mr. Jefferson's Bones.* This curious young scholar might open the lid, setting free the spirits of Thomas Jefferson and his beloved mammoth so they may drift through unknown territory, like smoke from ghostly campfires.

Thomas Jefferson has been called the Father of American Paleontology for his interest in prehistoric animals. Although he never went into the field to collect fossils, he devoted thirty years to encouraging the search for mastodon bones, organizing and funding expeditions. He risked his political career for science and was mocked by many people, including a thirteen-year-old boy who wrote a poem making fun of Jefferson's obsession.

To Jefferson, the creature represented all that was great about America—opportunity, discovery, and size. Jefferson shared his fossils and scientific information with scholars around the world. He was the first American to write a scientific paper on fossils, and in 1822, his "Great-claw" was officially named *Megalonyx jeffersonii.*

Science formed Jefferson's daily life. He kept a garden book and was happiest outdoors in the country. He carried a notebook, pencil, small telescope, compass, thermometer, pocketknife, and odometer (which measured distances) to capture his ideas and observations. He recorded the weather twice a day and even made notes on climate change, based on his record of snowfall in Virginia: "A change in our climate is taking place. . . . Both heats and colds are become much more moderate. . . . Snows are less frequent and less deep."

But although Jefferson championed learning and enlightenment—and wrote in the Declaration of Independence that "all men are created equal," with the right to "life, liberty, and the pursuit of happiness"— he was also a slave owner. Enslaved people—including children—worked on Jefferson's estate, mostly without pay, allowing him the freedom to pursue his interests. Jefferson was also the father of several children by his house slave Sally Hemings. These children became his house slaves. His farm in Virginia was home to much scientific inquiry, yet it was not a place of equality for all who lived there. Charles Willson Peale, with whom Jefferson collaborated on the mammoth skeleton, was a slave owner as well. His slave Moses Williams was present at the assembling of the skeleton and assisted in puzzling through how the bones should go together. Peale wrote in his diary that Williams's attempts were more successful than others': "he did more good in that way than any one among those employed in the work."

Jefferson considered the 1803 Louisiana Purchase a triumph for the United States. Most of that territory was owned by Native Americans. At that time, they lived in tribes, using huge areas of land as hunting grounds. Jefferson, along with other officials, felt the Native Americans wasted valuable territory. He believed they should learn to live in towns and grow crops instead of hunting. More white settlers were coming to America each day. They would want to settle on that land. Some Native Americans agreed to Jefferson's plan. But most did not.

After Jefferson retired from public office, his interest turned to the creation of the University of Virginia. He saw his school as a place "in which all the branches of science . . . should be taught in their highest degree."

Though Jefferson reached the highest office in the land—president of the United States—he never believed he knew all there was to know.